FORGIVENESS

God's Invitation To Share in His Heart

Jeff Smith

This book is dedicated to my
friend, Mrs. Edith Difato,
who for over 20 years has been a
witness of love and forgiveness

"FORGIVENESS"

God's Invitation To Share in His Heart

The Word Among Us

9639 Doctor Perry Road

Ijamsville, Maryland 21754

ISBN: 0-932085-18-0

© 1998 by The Word Among Us Press

Cover design by David Crosson

Made and printed in the United States of America.

The author wishes to thank Edward Thibault for contributing the chapter
entitled "Forgiveness & Healing."

Contents

Introduction

Many gospel stories speak of Jesus' willingness to forgive anyone who came to him. One woman was so moved by his mercy that she broke all conventions to express her love, kissing Jesus' feet and anointing him with costly perfume (Luke 7:36-50). A tax collector named Zacchaeus willingly returned all the money he had stolen—and more besides—because he experienced Jesus' compassion (19:1-10). In his own parables of the lost son (15:11-32) and the tax collector in the Temple (18:9-14), Jesus showed how ready God is to forgive his people.

As followers of Jesus, we are called to face the question of forgiveness within our own hearts. Because we live in a world filled with division and bitterness, we can find this call very difficult, if not impossible at times. Everywhere we turn, we hear of families broken apart by unforgiveness. We have become accustomed to the suffering of entire nations and ethnic groups caught in a cycle of oppression. In so many situations, vengeance seems the accepted course of action, and mercy is not even considered. How our world needs to taste the power of Jesus' forgiveness! This is the promise of the gospel, that the mercy we receive from Jesus has the power to soften our hearts and enable us to forgive even the most painful of situations.

In this little book, we will examine the need to receive God's mercy and the call to extend forgiveness to others. It is our hope at *The Word Among Us* that we all will experience great healing as we taste Jesus' mercy and offer it to others. Let us come before Jesus like the sinful woman and Zacchaeus and listen as he tells us: "Your many sins have been forgiven" (see Luke 7:47). As you meditate on these stories, allow Jesus to speak to you. Tasting his forgiveness and compassion, we will begin to forgive others with this same love.

Jeff Smith
The Word Among Us

"I Forgive You"

There is perhaps no statement more powerful than this. It carries with it a sense of generosity toward someone who has hurt us, a desire to see a wounded relationship healed, and—most powerfully—a sharing in the very nature of God, who is "slow to anger and abounding in steadfast love" (Psalm 103:8).

Yet, for all its power, this is often one of the most difficult statements to make. Lack of forgiveness has haunted humanity from the start, leaving its wounds in individuals, families, communities, and entire nations. Scripture tells of its effects in the story of Absalom and Amnon (2 Samuel 13-19) and in the tale of Joseph and his brothers (Genesis 37-46). Throughout his ministry, Jesus taught about the need to forgive fully (Matthew 6:14-15; 18:21-35; John 8:1-11) because he knew how prone we are to withhold mercy.

Forgiveness and the "Logic of Love"

Pope John Paul II has spoken of the urgent need for forgiveness: "Forgiveness can seem contrary to human logic, which often yields to the dynamics of conflict and revenge. But forgiveness is inspired by the logic of love, that love which God has for every man and woman" (Address for World Day of Peace, 1997, 1). These words seem so simple, yet our world is in such dire need for forgiveness and love. Even those who profess their faith in Christ can be lacking in mercy toward others. What is this "logic of love" to which the Holy Father refers? How does it differ from "human logic"?

To understand the "logic of love," one must know him who is love. This is crucial, because the ability to love and forgive is first and foremost something that God does in us. God is love itself (1 John 4:16), and as we yield and bind ourselves to him, we receive his love and find ourselves able to share that love with others. We forgive just as freely as we have been forgiven.

Do you know God as love? The more deeply we know God dwelling in our hearts, the more deeply the Holy Spirit will inspire us to grasp God's love and enable us to surpass the limitations of human reason. Certainly, logic is a wonderful gift from God that helps us to reason soundly and make right choices. However, by the power of the Holy Spirit, a relationship with God can take us beyond human capabilities and give us a share in God's own divine nature. We can actually become like him. Baptism is our first step in this transforming process. Every day we are called to further our knowledge and understanding of God's love poured into our hearts (Romans 5:5), until we reach the point where "God's forgiveness becomes in our hearts an inexhaustible source of forgiveness in our relationships with one another" (Pope John Paul II, World Day of Peace, 1).

The Divine Capacity To Love

In the New Testament, God revealed the infinite lengths to which his love would extend. Throughout his public ministry, Jesus offered love and forgiveness to those bound by sickness and sin. He welcomed outcasts lovingly, and public sinners found mercy and compassion in him. He even answered the pleas of Romans and Canaanites. Jesus Christ, the very image of the invisible God (Colossians 1:15), was so filled with his Father's love that he offered forgiveness and salvation to everyone he encountered (Luke 19:1-10), and it hurt him to see his gift of love rejected (Matthew 23:37-38).

Throughout his life, Jesus demonstrated the need to go beyond the human capacity to love. He taught us not to retaliate against those who hurt or persecute us, but to love them (Matthew 5:44). He manifested this love most perfectly at Calvary, where he poured out his very life so that we could receive God's forgiveness. As he hung there, with the nails piercing his hands and feet, he heard the crowds mocking him and the religious leaders taunting him to display his power.

Jesus knew he didn't deserve anything that he was enduring, yet he prayed: "Father, forgive them;

for they know not what they do" (Luke 23:34).
Jesus offered this prayer not only for those at
Golgotha on that first Good Friday—his forgiveness extends to every one of us. As his people,
filled with his Spirit, we can now rise above the
limitations of human logic and extend this same
love and forgiveness to anyone who has hurt us.

The Heart of the Problem

Even a superficial look at the world around us
reveals the immense need for forgiveness rooted in
the love of God. Violence and war have ravaged
countries for years, producing generations raised in
an atmosphere of hatred and vengeance. In the
developing world, hunger and starvation have
robbed entire nations of hope and reduced them to
a life-long struggle for survival. In the Western
world, few people have been spared the breakdown

of family life. Many have seen members of their own family wounded by divorce or infidelity. Reports of child abuse, runaway parents, and domestic violence are all around us. Without the gift of genuine forgiveness, these problems will continue to produce an ever-deepening atmosphere of guilt, isolation, and hatred.

Many people live under a tremendous burden of guilt because they don't know how to deal with the sins and temptations of daily life. Whether it is over major sins or minor transgressions, guilt robs us of the joy and freedom that is the rightful heritage of every Christian. When guilt is left to fester, it can lead to confusion, isolation, and even physical illness as it leaves a person bitter, defensive, and sapped of his or her self-esteem.

What is the answer to this plague of guilt? Jesus told his disciples: "As the Father has loved me, so have I loved you" (John 15:9). No matter our circumstances, our God is "merciful and gracious, slow to anger and abounding in steadfast love and faithfulness" (Exodus 34:6). Through the Holy Spirit, God has poured his love into our hearts (Romans 5:5), and it is there—in the depths of our being—that we can experience a divine forgiveness that melts away guilt and shame. At any moment, we can turn to God and know his love and forgiveness. He wants to pour out his mercy, and the only thing he looks for is a repentant heart.

As God's love is poured into our hearts, so much that we can almost feel it, we begin to sense that even we can have an effect on this plague of guilt and shame. Every day, we are called to love everyone around us—at home, in our neighborhoods, at work, and at school. The daily practice of forgiveness pleases God immensely, because it is a reflection of the mercy Jesus has for us. These personal situations may seem small when we compare them to the monumental problems facing humanity. Still, by bringing God's love and forgiveness to bear in our hearts and in our relationships, we allow the power of the gospel to change our lives and the lives of everyone around us. In his day, Jesus preached only in a few towns in Palestine, and yet his words changed the entire world. We, his followers, can do the same.

Jesus' love can release us from bondage to guilt on a daily basis. Every evening, before you go to bed, ask yourself: "How did I respond to difficult situations today—the little trials that tested my faith? How did these situations affect my relationship with the Lord and with those around me?" The gospel calls us first to confess our sins, accepting Jesus' forgiveness, and then to offer forgiveness to others and accept their forgiveness. By asking these few simple questions, we will begin to see significant changes in our lives.

God's Eagerness To Forgive

As Jesus becomes the foundation of our lives, we grasp more fully the love of God—a love so great that he gave up his beloved Son to win forgiveness for us. In the parable of the prodigal son (Luke 15:11-32), we can see the interplay between God's love and his desire to forgive. Even after the young man squandered everything, his father watched anxiously for his return. Finally catching sight of his lost son, the man ran to greet him, embraced him and showered him with kisses. In a similar way, God our Father runs to meet us and forgive us whenever we turn back to him. "He doesn't even let the son apologize: everything is forgiven. The intense joy of forgiveness, offered and received, heals seemingly incurable wounds, restores relationships and firmly roots them in God's inexhaustible love" (Pope John Paul II, World Day of Peace, 6).

"God is prepared to forgive me!" Nothing could be greater than this realization. God is so merciful that when we go to him, there is no bitterness, grudge, or resentment that might hinder him from pouring out his love. Just as Jesus washed his disciples' feet (John 13:1-15), he wants to wash our feet. So much did Jesus love his disciples that he willingly became their servant. The only greater expression of his love came on the following day when he hung on the cross to free us all from sin. Now, every day, he is prepared to wash our feet as we approach him in prayer, seek his presence at Mass, and listen to his word in scripture.

Pope John Paul II wrote: "The liberating encounter with forgiveness, though fraught with difficulties, can be experienced even by a wounded heart, thanks to the healing power of love, which has its first source in God" (World Day of Peace, 4). Have you ever had the experience in prayer of feeling so loved and forgiven by God that you couldn't even explain it—you just allowed his love to wash over you? It is this kind of experience that warms our hearts and enables us to love others. Let us open our hearts to receive his mercy every day. Let us ask him to make us as merciful and loving as he is.

In Jesus' Own Words

On Prayer and Forgiveness:

"Whenever you stand praying, forgive, if you have anything against anyone; so that your Father also who is in heaven may forgive you your trespasses."
(Mark 11:25)

As we extend blessing and forgiveness to others, God showers his mercy and forgiveness upon us.

On Mercy:

"Go and learn what this means: 'I desire mercy, and not sacrifice.' " (Matthew 9:13)

Some may think that enduring wounds inflicted on them in the past is the personal "cross" that they are to bear. But God is more pleased with mercy than sacrifice; he delights in seeing his children freed from past hurts as they learn to forgive.

On Unity and Division:

"Every kingdom divided against itself is laid waste, and no city or house divided against itself will stand." (Matthew 12:25)

The evil one seeks to divide relationships in our families, parishes, and among friends, causing our homes and our communities to crumble and be "laid waste." Repentance and forgiveness in our homes and in our parishes can conquer the power of evil, enabling us to stand firm in love.

Forgive as I Have
Forgiven You

The Key to Receiving God's Mercy

After proclaiming for three years that the kingdom of God was near, Jesus of Nazareth, an itinerant rabbi from Galilee, was executed by crucifixion at the hands of the Romans. Curious onlookers, hardened soldiers, and even religious leaders taunted him as he hung on the cross. Jesus knew he was innocent of the charges brought against him, yet despite the injustice of his death, he chose to offer mercy, not retaliation. He didn't even try to justify himself, but instead, he prayed: "Father, forgive them; for they know not what they do" (Luke 23:34).

A few years later, one of this man's disciples—Stephen—offered a similar prayer as he was being martyred: "Lord, do not hold this sin against them" (Acts 7:60). A zealous Pharisee named Saul heard this prayer and, upon his conversion, dedicated his life to spreading the good news of God's mercy and teaching others to extend this mercy to everyone around them.

Justice or Mercy?

More than anyone else, Jesus had a right to seek retribution against his accusers. Every day, he chose to love everyone he encountered—Jew or

Gentile, even the worst of sinners. He healed the sick, cast out demons, raised the dead, and fed the hungry. He spent his entire life joyfully serving his people. By all logic, such generosity and love should have been rewarded, not punished; he should have been honored and respected by all. Instead, he was slandered, plotted against, and ultimately executed. Yet it was in his willing sacrifice on the cross that Jesus revealed God's desire to forgive even the worst of sinners.

Similarly, Stephen could have reacted with a natural, human response to his executors. Had he been concerned only for his well-being, he would have been filled with fear and anger as the Jews began hurling stones at him. But Stephen's faith exceeded what his eyes could see or his mind could grasp. By faith, he fixed his eyes on Jesus and stayed close to him, even in this darkest of moments. Stephen had faith in a living God who commanded him to love even when persecuted, slandered, or physically abused.

Freely Give What You Have Freely Received

Jesus' command to love and forgive is not intended only for extreme situations like Stephen's. Jesus taught his disciples to forgive even the smallest of sins, and to forgive over and over, if necessary (Matthew 18:21-22). They were to forgive freely because they had been forgiven to a far greater degree. To illustrate his point, Jesus told a parable about a king's mercy toward his servant (18:23-35). This servant owed the king a debt so large that he could not possibly pay it off in his lifetime. Facing debtor's prison, he pleaded for more time so that he could pay what he owed. His plea for leniency so touched the king that he wrote off the debt completely, even though he had every right to sell the servant's family into slavery to recover at least part of it. The king's mercy triumphed over what would have been a just and legal course of action.

Having just been forgiven so great a debt, however, this man encountered a fellow servant who owed him a very small amount. He grabbed him by the throat, demanded immediate repayment, and had him thrown into prison. By law, he too had every right to do just as he did. But when the king heard about this, he summoned the servant and said to him: "You wicked servant! I forgave you all that debt because you besought me; and should not you have had mercy on your fellow servant, as I had mercy on you?" (Matthew 18:32-33). With that, he threw the man into prison.

It is because of his mercy that God has written off the immense debt of sin that each of us owes him. In justice, God has every right to condemn us for our sin rather than extend mercy. But in order to "write off" our debt, he sent his beloved Son to the cross to bear the punishment we deserved. As recipients of such abundant grace, we face the question of whether we will deal with others according to the mercy that we have freely received or according to the strict demands of justice. Jesus himself taught his disciples: "With the judgment you pronounce you will be judged, and the measure you give will be the measure you get" (Matthew 7:2). If we want to be treated mercifully, it is up to us to treat everyone else with mercy.

Obstacles to Forgiveness

This principle of mercy is simple to understand and yet difficult to practice in our day-to-day lives: I must forgive if I want to receive forgiveness (Matthew 6:14-15). This is partly due to the fact that society places a high value on the rights of the individual—often to the detriment of personal relationships. Imagine what a joyful and close family we would have if everyone were to embrace Jesus' command to forgive! How attractive the body of Christ would look if every brother and sister in the church forgave as God has forgiven us!

In order to take this commandment seriously, we must face the unforgiveness that remains within our hearts and ask God to teach us his way of mercy. There are many reasons why we might find it difficult to forgive; let's look at two of the most common.

He really isn't sorry, and I can't forgive him until he apologizes to me. Have you ever felt this way? Someone may have said or done something hurtful or cruel, something that wounded you to the heart. Perhaps this person purposely sought to hurt you and shows no regret. It may seem impossible—even unwise—to forgive such an act. But this was not Jesus' disposition. Confronted with the strongest hatred, opposition, and cruelty, he chose to extend love and mercy.

I have neither the power nor the desire to forgive that person. Whatever the situation, we face a choice: Trusting in the power of God to change our hearts, we can obey Jesus' command to love; or, we can succumb to the feelings of frustration and bitterness that seek to rule us. As we appeal to our faith in God and his commands, choosing to offer forgiveness freely and without conditions, God will bring about a gradual change in us, empowering us to be as merciful as he is (Luke 6:36).

Freedom through Forgiveness

Experience tells us that every day, we face many "little" situations in which we are called to offer and seek forgiveness. Our spouse may do something that irritates or angers us. We may lose our temper with one of our children or a co-worker. If we take just a couple of minutes to review a typical day, we will probably find several situations in which mercy and forgiveness could warm our hearts with God's peace and joy. These small circumstances are sometimes the hardest things to forgive, but as we forgive—even the smallest hurt—we open our lives to immense change and blessing.

Jesus' first concern is that we learn to forgive from the heart (Matthew 18:35). When thoughts of anger and tension against someone rise up in us, we have a wonderful opportunity to become more like our Master. We can choose to forgive and bless that person by asking God to pour his love out upon him or her. Such a prayer is powerful enough to unlock the chains of bitterness within our own hearts and send blessings to those who have hurt us. Our heavenly Father especially loves this prayer because it is the way that Jesus prayed.

Some relationships may be so damaged that actual reconciliation may not be possible. In these cases, God still asks us to forgive from the heart, even if we have been deeply wronged. In the presence of our God, who knows our hearts, we can honestly acknowledge how deeply we have been hurt, choose to forgive those who hurt us, and ask God to bless them. In other situations, we may have the opportunity to verbalize our forgiveness and blessing. It is truly beautiful to be able to tell someone who has hurt us: "I forgive you and I love you." Nothing frees up a relationship more than hearing such words. This is why it is vital that we teach our children the practice of forgiving one another in an open and loving environment.

We should also recognize that when we do forgive others, we may or may not experience a sense

of peace and reconciliation. Tension may remain;
we may still feel uncomfortable around certain
people. But this should not discourage us. We have
not forgiven in order to reduce tension. We forgive
because Jesus has called us to be like him. Through
the power of his Spirit at work within us, we can
choose to love and bless, even in the face of tension or hardness of heart. There is no greater priv-
ilege than becoming like Jesus, our merciful and
loving Master.

Meeting the Lord of the Cross

From the time of his conversion, and for the rest of his life, St. Ignatius of Loyola made a regular habit of prayerfully reading the gospel accounts of Jesus' passion. Through this practice, Ignatius came into contact with Jesus in an intimate and vibrant way that sustained him and comforted him in every situation.

In a similar way, we want to draw near to Jesus, who overcame all sin and broken relationships when he offered up his life at Calvary. As many days as possible this month, read small portions of the passion narratives and ponder the love and compassion that drew Jesus to Calvary. In exercises such as these, we can know Jesus' presence more deeply and experience his power that enables us to forgive others with the same love and mercy with which he has forgiven us.

Forgiveness & Healing

Throughout his public ministry, Jesus pro-
claimed the good news of salvation, and he
demonstrated his ability to save by healing
the sick wherever he went (Matthew 4:23; 9:1-7;
Luke 7:19-22). Now risen in glory, Jesus' desire to
save his people has not changed, and neither has
his ability to cast out sickness and disease. Jesus
wants to heal his people of their illnesses. He wants
to show us mercy, and all he asks is that we forgive

others from the heart, just as he has forgiven us. Learning how to be generous with others shows us how generous God is with us and increases our faith in his ability to heal us, both spiritually and physically. In this chapter, we look at how showing mercy to those who have hurt us opens the door for us to receive mercy and healing from our heavenly Father.

> *The prayer of faith will save the sick man, and the Lord will raise him up; and if he has committed sins, he will be forgiven. Therefore confess your sins to one another, and pray for one another, that you may be healed. (James 5:15-16)*

This connection between forgiveness and healing that the letter of James describes so wonderfully can be a difficult concept to understand. People with terminal illnesses, for example, could feel doubly chastised, thinking that the reason they have not been healed is that they still harbor unrepented sins or unforgiveness in their hearts. That would imply that it was their own fault that they have not been healed.

Eye for Eye

Part of our problem in grasping the connection between forgiveness and healing is that our thinking can be imbued with a harsh sense of retributive justice. We might think that God cannot—or will not—simply forgive sins, that he has to mete out a punishment that befits the crime. This was the Old Testament teaching that Jesus referred to when he said: "You have heard that it was said, 'An eye for an eye and a tooth for a tooth.' But I say to you, Do not resist one who is evil. But if any one strikes you on the right cheek, turn to him the other also" (Matthew 5:38-39; see Leviticus 24:19-21).

Jesus taught us to move from the level of retribution to the level of mercy—for our own good as well as for the sake of those we are called to forgive. Retributive justice works like a two-edged sword: As long as we insist on retribution for the evil done to us, we will find it hard to accept God's unconditional forgiveness of our sin against him. And, by closing ourselves off to his mercy, we close ourselves off to his desire to heal us simply because he loves us.

From Retribution to Redemption

Although this kind of retributive justice permeates much of the Old Testament, there are also constant reminders that God's ways are not our ways (Isaiah 55:8-9; Hosea 11:9; Psalm 103:8-10). As we survey the Old Testament we can see how the more ancient concept of retributive justice gradually gave way to a deeper understanding of

God's mercy, opening the door for the redemptive justice that pervades the New Testament.

Jesus showed his disciples the indispensable nature of forgiveness when he taught them to pray: "Forgive us our debts, as we also have forgiven our debtors" (Matthew 6:12). Throughout his ministry, Jesus linked forgiveness with healing: "Which is easier, to say, 'Your sins are forgiven,' or to say, 'Rise and walk'? But that you may know that the Son of man has authority on earth to forgive sins"—he then said to the paralytic—"Rise, take up your bed and go home" (Matthew 9:5-6). Jesus even made forgiveness and reconciliation a prerequisite to worship: "If you are offering your gift at the altar, and there remember that your brother has something against you, leave your gift there before the altar and go; first be reconciled to your brother, and then come and offer your gift" (Matthew 5:23-24).

The connection between forgiveness and healing was clear to Jesus. To us, however, the idea of retributive justice—that people must pay for their offenses without any hope for mercy—runs deep. It is a major factor in the support of capital punishment. For some, it may also be an element in the line of reasoning that asserts that our good deeds can earn us salvation. More subtly, it may even influence those whose goal is to please Jesus. Of course, desiring to please the Lord is a beautiful thing; we should all be trying to please him. But we put limits on God's love when we think that the more we please God, the more he will love us, and the more disposed he will be to reward us with eternal life.

All these kinds of thoughts make God's love dependent on what we do, as if our actions determine our salvation. We can see this in recent surveys of Catholics which found that about 70 percent of average parishioners and 85 percent of teenagers believed that it is by their own efforts that they earn a place in heaven. God loves us when we do something good, but he loves sinners also—even though the sin itself is abhorrent to him. Jesus himself said that he came to save sinners, not "the righteous" (Mark 2:17). We are the sinners he came to save (Romans 3:23; *Catechism of the Catholic Church*, 543-545).

Forgiveness, God's Gift of Healing

As we freely accept God's forgiveness and freely forgive those who have hurt us, we open ourselves to the healing power of God. This is because such free forgiveness involves a sharing in the very life of God. We don't forgive because we are good people; we forgive because God's grace—his life within us—enables us to become like him. His forgiveness and mercy are total and perfect, flooding us like a mighty river.

Gracious Father that he is, God wants to heal us totally, to free us from everything that holds us in bondage. We, however, can be selective in our desire for healing. The healing we ask of God is often quite different from the healing he wants to give us. We will gladly be freed of that pain in our knee, but we might still want to hold on to the anger in our heart—because the one who caused us to be angry deserves our wrath. We may reason that if only this or that pain were to disappear, all would be well. But God knows that if we can be set free of the unforgiveness in our hearts, our pain will disappear or be more easily borne.

Most of us carry around wounds and scars—physical, emotional, or spiritual—from broken relationships, painful memories, wounds within our families, physical ailments, sins that we cannot forgive or that we think God cannot forgive. A lack of forgiveness can cause, prolong, or reopen many of these wounds. This is why Jesus taught that if we are to receive daily forgiveness of our trespasses, it will come as we forgive those who have trespassed against us. The Lord's Prayer is so familiar to us that we may tend to overlook the sobering fact that we are asking God to forgive us in the same way that we forgive others.

If God were a retributive judge, waiting to catch us in some wrongdoing, he could trap us in these very words. God knows that we sometimes harbor unforgiveness, even when we are praying to be forgiven or healed. He still offers us his mercy if we forgive as he has forgiven us. He wants to free us of our unforgiveness so that we can be totally healed. Because God respects the precious gift of our free will, however, he waits for us to choose to be freed by our freely forgiving others.

Sowing and Reaping

Scripture teaches us that we reap what we sow (Galatians 6:7). If we sow bitterness, anger, and resentments, we will reap the same harvest in our lives. Satan—the accuser of God's people (Revelation 12:9-10)—can be subtle, but he is deadly as he looks for a foothold of unforgiveness in our hearts. We may end up getting for ourselves just what we wished upon others . . . and that can be sobering and frightening. On the other hand, if we sow a crop of forgiveness and mercy, we allow Jesus to protect us from the evil one; we clear the way for the Spirit to wash us in the healing blood of Jesus. Then we can rejoice, because in God's mercy we have been healed and are now able to forgive others even more freely.

Scripture also teaches us that "he who sows sparingly will also reap sparingly, and he who sows bountifully will also reap bountifully" (2 Corinthian 9:6). Sowing forgiveness is not something we do quickly . . . one time, and then it's over. We must sow and overseed. Every day, we should ask the Spirit to reveal deeper areas of unforgiveness in us so that we can continually be filled with healings of spirit, soul, and body.

God wants to heal and restore all of his people. But self-inflicted wounds of unforgiveness create barriers that prevent his healing power from flowing freely. How he wants us to understand the magnitude of his mercy! How he wants to show us that whatever retribution his justice required has been paid for by the blood of his beloved Son! We did not make—nor could we ever have made—reparation for our sins. But out of his love for us, God has won our forgiveness. How, then, can we withhold forgiveness from anyone for any sin? May the Holy Spirit inspire us to forgive as we have been forgiven.

Then the flood of God's healing power will wash away all our wounds and scars.